Motivation And Productivity Guide

Find Methods For Self-Motivation, Time Planning, Goal Achieving And Personal Productivity

Text Copyright © Matthew Wright

All rights reserved. No part of this guide may be reproduced in any form without permission in writing from the publisher except in the case of brief quotations embodied in critical articles or reviews.

Legal & Disclaimer

The information contained in this book and its contents is not designed to replace or take the place of any form of medical or professional advice; and is not meant to replace the need for independent medical, financial, legal or other professional advice or services, as may be required. The content and information in this book have been provided for educational and entertainment purposes only.

The content and information contained in this book have been compiled from sources deemed reliable, and it is accurate to the best of the Author's knowledge, information, and belief. However, the Author cannot guarantee its accuracy and validity and cannot be held liable for any errors and/or omissions. Further, changes are periodically made to this book as and when needed. Where appropriate and/or necessary, you must consult a professional (including but not limited to your doctor, attorney, financial advisor or such other professional advisor) before using any of the suggested remedies, techniques, or information in this book.

Upon using the contents and information contained in this book, you agree to hold harmless the Author from and against any damages, costs, and expenses, including any legal fees potentially resulting from the application of any of the information provided by this book. This disclaimer applies to any loss, damages or injury caused by the use and application, whether directly or indirectly, of any advice or information presented, whether for breach of contract, tort, negligence, personal injury, criminal intent, or under any other cause of action. You agree to accept all risks of using the information presented in this book.

You agree that by continuing to read this book, where appropriate and/or necessary, you shall consult a professional (including but not limited to your doctor, attorney, or financial advisor or such other advisor as needed) before using any of the suggested remedies, techniques, or information in this book.

Table of Contents

Introduction 6
Part 1. Understanding the Connection – Motivation and Productivity 7
    What is Motivation? 7
    What is Productivity? 9
    Why Do We Lose Motivation? 11
    Motivation and Productivity - Relationship 17
    Research and Studies 19
Part 2. You Can Make a Difference 20
    Be Your Own Champion-Motivate Yourself 20
    Don't Be Afraid To Ask For Help 27
    Success Story – Jack Ma 28
    KFC – Success Story 30
Part 3. Start your journey to a happy you 31
    Happiness is the Key 31
    Take Baby Steps 33
    Start Planning and Get Organized 36
Part 4. Frist Thing's First 39
    Set Your Goals 39
    Make a To-Do List 42
Part 5. Hacks for Staying Happy, Motivated, and Productive 46
Conclusion 50

Introduction

Do you often feel you lack motivation and have no energy to accomplish anything despite so much of that is waiting for you?

Then you try to push yourself, make a list of tasks, but it simply doesn't work. You spend hours watching TV or surfing through social networks. Then you beat up yourself for such behaviour and try to change it from tomorrow.

The next day, with the same old to-do list, you procrastinate again, while others seem organized and managing everything, not only usual everyday chores, but great careers, hobbies, family, and me-time. How do they do that?

This book is what you need. Here you will find out how to become one of those happy, successful people, who seem always to be enthusiastic and productive.

There are many methods, tools, and strategies, which will help you, become and stay motivated forever. Try out all of them or choose those that seem right for you.

Part 1. Understanding the Connection – Motivation and Productivity

What is Motivation?

Have you ever wondered what power makes someone waking up at 5 a.m. every single morning and work out, while someone spends his life on a couch? What makes people work long hours and take night classes while others can't wait to finish a day at work and go home?

Motivation is the key. That power inspires people to move toward their goals. It involves all the reasons for someone's behaviour and actions. The word motivation is derived from the word motive, which means desires, drives, and causes of someone's actions.

Motivation is one of the most crucial reasons for behaviour, so it's not surprising there are many psychological theories made about it. We'll mention some of them, just to understand better the importance of motivation.

What the thing about all the theories agrees is that humans have some general needs, which must be satisfied. Our motivation could be a positive one- to reach satisfaction or negative - to avoid some unpleasant consequence. That works on the principle of reward and punishment. From an early age, people learn to behave the specific way to deserve some reward or to avoid punishment.

Our behaviour can determine our needs, which can be primitive, elemental, like food, water, and shelter, or more sophisticated and social oriented, like acceptance, love or recognition. These are rewards to our pleasure center in our brains. It can be money, grades, or achieving some goals.

If we simplify things, those are all rewards. Any unpleasant feelings - hunger, thirst, loneliness, misery, poverty and so on- can be considered punishment. That's the primary basis of the answer what drives people toward through life.

Our motivation for doing something can be intrinsic, which means that a person has internal willpower, desire for some action, which brings him personal joy as a reward. The other kind of motivation is extrinsic rewards - people often do what is needed to win wage or grades, others attention, recognition, and love.

Our desires make us give the best of ourselves and achieve almost anything. A desire is what makes a person do his best, something that makes an effort worth doing. Stronger desire gives us stronger motivation.

Taking any action demands motivation; you need it to begin, to continue, and to finish. You need both short and long-term motivation. Taking the first step is essential, but you need to make every other step to get to the end, too.

What is Productivity?

Although we all have the same amount of time, 24 hours a day, 365 days a year, some people manage to make more things done in a couple of hours than the others do for the whole day in the office.

Productivity is the ability to work efficiently. Quick working makes you use the maximum of the time you have and helps you boost the results.

The difference in people's productivity comes from a mix of factors. Motivation is the most significant of them. Then there comes the difference in a level of talent, work environment, the ability of self-discipline and time management. Sometimes even the luck may be the factor that makes the difference.

Some people seem to be naturally talented to be super-productive, while others make some effort to accomplish daily habits to help themselves in work efficiency.

First, there is no productivity without proper motivation. If you know the reason why you do something, you are motivated and ready to do what is needed to succeed. Finding your "why," your life calling and purpose of your efforts make your work has sense. It's excellent motivation to feel useful and appreciated. Other kinds of motives are valuable, too. It doesn't matter if you work to afford abundance, or to make this world a better place. The thing is that you know your big "why." Finding a broad meaning in what you do boosts your productivity.

Motivation will get you started and help you gain momentum, but remember that motivation is temporary. You are the one who will need to motivate yourself when you feel a lack of willpower. You must decide to continue. Motivation is not endless, but your reason for acting will keep you productive.

Productivity is all about overcoming procrastination, its biggest enemy. It's about being enterprising, using motivation to start, and then keep your focus on purpose and direction. It's about using your time wisely and get the maximum from your work.

Highly productive people have better chances to achieve their goals. They are more successful overall. They are also often happier, because they know how to set priorities and are good at time management. That makes them enjoy the fullness of life while adding actual value to the world.

Why Do We Lose Motivation?

Almost everyone experiences a lack of enthusiasm and motivation from time to time. It can show up in every field of our lives - in work, relationships, everyday life. The lack of motivation can cause dissatisfaction and indifference. People react to this situation differently. Some of them are giving up their goals, both short- and long-term, while others are struggling to move on although unmotivated. Loss of motivation causes laziness; procrastination becomes a habit and makes you feel an absence of energy.

If you have lost enthusiasm to follow goals, you can't blame anyone. But what you need to do is finding a way to motivate yourself. It's crucial to awake motivation and enthusiasm if you wish to improve your life. You need the drive to follow your dreams, but also to do everyday chores and tasks. Life is much more incredible when you have incentives and purpose.

There are many reasons why our enthusiasm fades. Most of them are internal and personal, but there can be a few external factors, too. What can you do? To start, you should become aware of the reasons for the loss of motivation and understand that you have the power to change your mental programming. Some of these reasons include the following:

1. Lack of Confidence in Your Abilities

When a person underestimates own abilities and thinks about itself as no good enough, there's no much space for motivation. Self-confidence is crucial for achieving the goals. If someone thinks he's not able to follow own dreams, there's no point to acting. In this case, a person should do on self-confidence and real abilities first. That will boost energy and awake motivation.

2. Fear of Failure

This kind of fear in inherent to humans and it's precious in healthy doses. It makes us awaken and aware of possible dangers. Thinking your boat is unsinkable will lead you nowhere. But now we are talking about the other, unhealthy fear of failure, which paralyzes. Sometimes it can be so intense that one's giving up. It's better not to try at all, than experience that scary scenario. The cure for this is to stop catastrophizing and accepting failure as a natural part of the learning process.

3. Inaction, Laziness, Procrastination

The motivation is what you need for action. But, if you don't take any action, the rush of motivation won't visit you quite often. No matter what stands in your way, be it fear or other obstacles, you need to take action. Laziness is not an excuse. It might be the smallest reason, but it is still wide-spread. Get rid of it. Now. Don't even consider it as a valuable reason.

Procrastination is the most examined and talked about as a motivation killer. Researchers found a strong correlation between procrastination and fear of failure. If you have a habit of delaying tasks and wasting time meanwhile instead of being productive, that's a particular problem for itself, and you should put some effort into solving it.

4. Lacking Purpose, Loss of Meaning

You can't maintain motivation if you don't really care about what you're doing. You need to find the meaning. Why is it important? How does it help others? Selfish oriented goals have fewer chances to be achieved than those oriented on helping others. If you believe you bring value to the world and help people, you'll be more enthusiastic. Providing for your dear ones, for example, is an excellent motive for work. So, find your "why" and keep it on the mind.

5. Lack of Focus or Direction

The focus is a powerful tool. They say that energy flows where the attention goes. Be wise with using your focus and direct your attention on purpose. Keep an eye on the goal, know your "why," and go straight. Do what is needed now, so you will be free to do what you want later. Put all of your attention on what you are doing now. That way, you'll be motivated, focused, fearless, and productive.

Don't lose your internal compass. You know where you want to get, so keep the destination on your mind. Following the decided direction makes things easier. Only that way will bring you where you wanted, so don't lose the path or change it whenever you face some obstacle.

6. Unclear Priorities

There will always be many other activities, movies to watch, coffees to sipping with friends, dirty dishes, full laundry baskets. It's up to you to set the priorities. You are the one who should make some time for the activities that will lead you closer to your goals. Then you have to protect that time and save it exclusively for those activities. If there are always other more important things to do, examine your goals again. Maybe you don't want that much what you say you desire. Perhaps it's just not a priority for you. It's all about priorities.

7. Feeling Entitled

Are you may be one of those people who believe they are born to be successful? If so, there's nothing inherently wrong with that as long as you work hard. However, in general, people who believe they are meant to succeed have the feeling that the world owes them something, and everyone should know how special they are. They are easy to discourage when their effort isn't immediately and adequately rewarded.

8. Impatience, Expecting Immediate Results

Daydreaming and visualizing wanted scenario is nice, but unrealistic expectations are not. If you expect to grow rich opening your new store, that's a challenging, long-term goal. However, if you hope it to happen immediately, in a few months, then you need to put your feet on the ground. Otherwise, you'll feel disappointed and may give up. The cure is to learn how to set short-term and long-term goals, to be patient and have faith in the process.

9. Inflexibility

If you are stubborn and insist everything must go exactly the way you think it should, there are big chances for disappointment. That way you are likely to lose enthusiasm and give up if everything is not as you like. If you are stubborn and insist everything must go exactly the way you think it should, there are big chances for disappointment. That way you are likely to lose enthusiasm and give up if everything is not as you like. Accept that things are always happening for our highest good and give up on holding the belief there is only one way to succeed.

10. Working Too Hard

Being an eager beaver and giving your best is the recipe for high achievement, but working too hard and disregard other life fields is a bad idea. If you leave yourself with too little rest, soon you will feel tired and unmotivated. Be wise when dosing your efforts to avoid burnout. The point is to work smart, not hard.

11. Setting Unrealistic Goals

The goal must be right-sized to keep us motivated. Too low makes us bored, while too high makes us disappointed and motivation fades away.

12. Fear of Other's Opinions

If you continuously think about other's opinion, you waste the energy. Everyone has a different point of view according to experience, emotions, and values. So, don't try to please everyone. Focus on what is important to you and on your "why."

13. Being Stressed or Nervous

Stress affects us in every possible way, so it's not surprising that it has an impact on our performance, too. Stress sets us on a surviving mode, and there's no space for motivation and productivity. Learn how to relax and when you feel nervous, make a pause from any task until you feel inner peace again.

14. Fear of Taking Risk

A risk is an inevitable part of every constructive action. Don't let it paralyze you. Take it as a challenge and enjoy playing the game.

15. Lack of Resources

This could be really frustrating. After spending ages searching for information you need for a project, it's disappointing to have not enough resources. No matter how motivated you have been, it expires rapidly. The same is true about money - lack of it kills all the ideas, enthusiasm and motivation, making everything hardly possible. Solutions are many, but it all starts with fixing your current financial situation. The motivation for that you can easily find in many ideas waiting for the resources.

16. Lack of Feedback

If you don't get feedback on what you are doing and don't know if you are going the right way, you will hardly put an extra effort, because you don't know if it's an investment or a waste.

17. Lack of Knowledge

If you find out you know a little about the subject, it's demotivating. Knowing more about something by the rule makes you want to know even more. Make lack of knowledge works for you - not to stop you, but to accelerate your effort toward learning.

18. Lack of Social Support System

It's very motivating if you have your own crowd supporting your back. But more important is to be yourself the most significant and most reliable support. That way, you don't depend on other's opinion and have the power to encourage and motivate yourself on your own.

Motivation and Productivity - Relationship

Motivation and productivity are twin concepts, they go hand in hand, and this relationship was the object of many pieces of research. Motivation has a significant influence on one's productivity. According to most studies, there is a positive correlation between these two - when motivation increases, we could expect productivity to rise. It's a direct cause and effect relationship. This correlation is natural, almost obvious.

If you want to be more efficient and productive, you will need positive motivation. The same case is if you are a leader who wants his employees to be more proactive. We'll consider both cases.

Lack of motivation causes poor performance, far below one's abilities. If not motivated, you'll find yourself bored, tired, without any wish to get up and welcome a new day. You may feel indifferent and disappointed. When not adequately motivated, we are more likely to procrastinate and waste our time on task of minor importance. If this repeat often, people often happen to think that they are not a good fit for the job, they are not good enough if not capable of being disciplined. That leads to giving up. Others decide to move on, despite lack of motivation. That becomes an everyday struggle to do what they have to. If they don't find a way to awake motivation and enthusiasm, what's coming is a burnout, not caused by hard work, but by self-dictatorship.

What you need is a pause. Take some time for yourself and use it for self-reflection. First, you need to find the root of the problem - the reason why you are short of motivation. Use the above list of possible causes. Maybe some of these reasons for lack of motivation appeals to you. If not, perhaps it can inspire you to find out what's that holding you from being enthusiastic.

When you dig out the reason why your motivation faded away, the cure will be apparent. This book will also help you in bringing back that sparkle of readiness to follow your dreams. Read on for many ways to awake lost enthusiasm.

If you are a leader or manager with the responsibility to motivate a team but only see absent people who are apathetic about productivity, don't despair. Imagine yourself in their shoes. Why should they bother? Are they getting enough in return? The truth is that nobody can motivate another. However, a person can be an inspiration for others. That way, they will want to make changes needed to become motivated. So, start with yourself. You are the one who should serve as an example of how you want your employees to behave.

Your example and inspiration are not enough. You need to use strategies appealed to both, the internal and external motivation of your employees. External factors of motivation would be salary, money bonuses, paid vacation, money rewards. You'll provide internal motivation if you offer them enough opportunities for self-growth, and show how their effort is appreciated. Showing gratitude is extremely powerful, also recognition, and a friendly work atmosphere. Those are some of the factors that affect motivation and productivity. Together, they bring results.

Research and Studies

A group of authors from Bangladesh University - Naby-Islam-Dip-Hossain, did scientific research in 2017 "Impact of Motivation on Employee Performances: A Case Study of Karmangsthan Bank Limited, Bangladesh." This research was a study on how motivational tools impacted the performance of employee for betterment. They took into account all known kinds of motivation and inferred to the conclusion that motivation indeed has a momentous effect on employee performance, and this connection is natural and obvious. In another study by Professor Eugenio Proto from University of Warwick, UK, and IZA, Germany, named "Are Happy Workers More Productive?", he offered pieces of evidence and concluded that happiness motivates greater effort, increasing output without affecting its quality and thus boosting productivity.

Part 2. You Can Make a Difference

Be Your Own Champion-Motivate Yourself

It would be nice to have someone behind you who continuously push you toward your goals, doesn't let you give up and motivate you when it's needed. But, as nobody can motivate others, you have to be that person for yourself. Don't worry about your productivity. Just find the way to awake motivation, and you'll see changes in efficiency. There are some proven ways to motivate yourself. Believe you can do it.

First, or even before anything else, this is the crucial thing. If you don't believe you can succeed, there's no point in taking action. You have a power within you, power to focus and direct your energy and effort. If you do it wisely, nothing is impossible to achieve. Remind yourself why you want to do something. If you keep your "why" on the mind, that gives you spiritual force and drive you forward. You are motivated, focused, and ready to take any action required when you remain where you want to get. A useful way to remind yourself of that is to build a vision board. Find pretty pictures that represent a life you want to live and place them together in a visible place. Every look at your vision board will motivate you in just a moment.

Remind yourself of what you are moving away from

Negative motivation is still motivation. Think about penalties and consequences of staying where you already are. That will also bring wind to your wings.

Focus on emotions

Why do we make goals and then procrastinate? It's because we make plans, but do not consider the impact of one huge factor - our emotions. The emotions are the central power that leads our behavior. So, don't suppress your feelings. Be aware of them, accept them and include in your plans. That way, there are more chances for realistic expectations and long-lasting motivation.

Get positive

We have the lowest motivation when we are in a bad mood. On the other hand, the highest motivation we feel in a positive state of mind. That's why, besides all the benefits from positive thinking, it has a significant impact on our productivity. You need to get positive. The good news is that you can learn how to practice that. In this book, you will find useful ways and suggestions on how to maintain a positive approach to life.

Get optimistic

Looking through an optimistic lens makes life seems brighter. Belief everything is good and will be even better makes you wish to put an effort in reaching your desires. Optimism and enthusiasm are also twin concept, just like motivation and productivity. Maintain optimism to stay motivated.

Reward yourself

We have already said how important feelings are for the motivation. Moreover, isn't enthusiasm a feeling itself? Rewards feel good. That's why it works. So, promise yourself a reward when you finish work. That way, even if the task is not pleasant, you will have something to look forward to.

Visualize yourself as a motivated, productive person

It's a fantastic tool for reaching anything. If you can already see yourself clearly as a successful, motivated, happy and productive person, there are big chances for that daydream to turn into reality. Let your imagination free, enjoy this vision, try to feel it as it's already here.

Surround yourself with the right people

The people with whom you spend your time matters. The vibration of people in your life becomes your vibration, too. So, choose wisely your circle. Enthusiastic and positive friends will influence you, and it will be easier to stay motivated.

A little bit of pressure can help

Pressure is often presented in a negative context. But it can be helpful in healthy doses. If you tell your friends and family about your goals and what you are doing, you will be less likely to procrastinate or give up. Even better if you can commit someone that you are going to succeed. This kind of pressure will hold you on the path.

Get inspired by people's success

You can find inspiration everywhere. That doesn't have to be someone from your social circle. There are numerous success stories from people worldwide, and you can find tons of books, videos, documentary movies, and stories to get inspired by others success.

Break down your work into smaller segments

A huge and important task ahead of you can make you feel overwhelmed, even without hard work. Divide it into smaller parts, and finish them one by one. That way you don't need the motivation to last long enough to complete the whole project. It's enough to be motivated to finish a part. Before you lose enthusiasm, the entire project is completed.

Make your activities fun

No one enjoys doing boring things. So make it fun if you want to stay motivated. For example, if you don't like to exercise, find some sports activity which entertains you, like boxing, dancing, or whichever is interesting to you.

Mix things up

Varying activities you do and finding a new input will increase motivation. Routine is killing it. So, change activities and variate ways you do them, listen to new podcasts, read new books, make it different.

Give yourself breaks

Hard work is appreciated, but if you don't make pauses, you will soon find yourself exhausted and with no more motivation.

Reduce distractions

If there are many things to distract you, you won't be concentrated and usually productive. Reduce as many distractors from your work environment as you can.

Create a routine

If you have a routine, you put less effort into thinking what to do next or when you are going to finish some tasks. That's why it's important to find the right schedule for yourself and stick to it. The other way a routine could help you is to make up your rituals, which would be signs and triggers for starting the work. It should be something simple, like drinking a glass of water, or preparing the tools you use. Something so simple you can't say no to.

Start small

Just start; it's crucial to keep moving. If a big goal makes you feel anxious, or a big task makes you procrastinate, start small. It's easier to find enthusiasm for a small step. If it still seems overwhelming, change it for an even smaller one.

Play music

Cheerful rhythm leaves no one bored or grumpy. It's also known as a powerful way to wake up the motivation for any work. So, let the music play, and the rhythm drives you.

Be kind to yourself

Self-dictatorship is a motivation-killer. Be kind to yourself as you would be to a friend. And if you fail, be gentle and compassionate.

Change your approach to failure

Instead of fear of failure, accept that as a natural part of learning and growing process. Don't waste your energy on negative emotions. It's perfectly normal to make mistakes. It shouldn't keep you from acting.

Compare yourself only to yourself

Instead of demotivating comparing to others, focus on measuring your progress. Compare yourself to yourself from past and notice how far you have come. That could be incredibly motivating.

Be grateful

Gratitude is a magical cure. Focus on what you already have and count your blessings. Be thankful for the path that brought you to this point, and for where you are now. Being grateful motivates you for bringing more things to your life which you would be thankful for.

Declutter and tidy up

Spend some time to make your workspace a place where it's a

pleasure to work. Minimalism and tidiness make it easier to concentrate on important tasks. You'll feel energized after a break for cleaning.

Reduce your to-do list

Just the sight of a long to-do list can make you feel overwhelmed. Try to shrink it to just one, most significant task. You'll find out how it feels to check as done all from your list. Prepare in advance the other list, with the second task, but keep it out of sight.

Make custom-sized goals

If the goal you have set scares you, set a smaller, or even a tiny one. Achieving it will help you build self-confidence and make you ready for bigger ones. If the goal you have set scares you, set a smaller, or even a tiny one. Achieving it will help you build self-confidence and make you ready for bigger ones. You need to find the perfect size for your goals, big enough to attract you, but not so big as to make you feel anxious.

Exercise

Working out, even something light as stretching, will make your blood circulating, and motivation will follow.

Reward yourself and celebrate

Keep the promise you have given yourself earlier and reward yourself for successfully finishing a task. Celebrate every success adequately; you deserve it.

Meditate

If you think you don't have time for meditation, think again. That time spent in meditation will turn out to be the best investment. Your productivity will amazingly improve. So, sit or lay still, concentrate on breathing. There are a dozen ways to meditate; you need to find the best for you.

Go outside

If nothing goes well, go for a walk. You'll come back refreshed, with new energy and ideas.

Just get started; don't wait for motivation to show up

Many people wait for something to happen to take action. That's a typical kind of procrastination. Don't let yourself wait for the motivation to show up. If you feel a lack of enthusiasm, start despite it. Let the motivation to keep up with you.

Don't Be Afraid To Ask For Help

Do you have a feeling that no matter how hard you are trying, things don't go as you want? It feels awful that whatever you do, it won't change anything. If you have tried everything, but nothing made a difference, don't hesitate to ask for help. It's not a shame; everybody happens to feel stuck from time to time.

Taking responsibility for your life is crucial for well-being. But it doesn't mean you always have to do everything on your own. Sometimes, the most responsible decision is to search for help. Recognizing that you need it, and asking for it can be the first step to a significant change.

If you have tried everything you could, but nothing helped, consider the idea of talking to an expert. Depression can be the cause for lack of motivation, and that's not the same as laziness or being temporarily unmotivated. That's not something you should ignore ignore, because no one should go through it alone.

Even if your loss of enthusiasm has nothing to do with depression, support is what you need if it lasts for some time. Most people need some help from the outside to get or stay motivated. That's why there are so many professionals out there, whose job is to offer support and help people find constructive ways to improve their lives. There are motivational speakers, motivational coaches, psychologists, and many others.

Nothing's wrong with you; you are not lazy, spoiled, weak or ill if you need some help. Perhaps you just need someone to help you find your own direction or the right way to do things.

Success Story – Jack Ma

Have you heard of Jack Ma? He is the richest man in China. He's also loved, and crowds of people come to listen to his speeches. However, that wasn't always the case. Jack Ma was born in 1964, in a poor Chinese family. He spent his childhood like all the Chinese kids. As a teenager, Ma offered visitors tours through the Hangzhou, his home city, in exchange for English lessons. That's how he got the nickname Jack. After finishing high school, he wanted to go to college but failed the entrance exam - twice. He didn't give up, and finally passed on the third time, and graduated in 1988. That was just a beginning. He started to apply to as many jobs as he could but was rejected a dozen times. When he finally found a job as an English teacher, his salary was only $12 per month. During a visit to the US in 1995, Ma was amazed by the internet and its possibilities. His first online search was "beer," and the results were surprising for him - there was not any Chinese beer in the results. It in that moment, he decided to change that. He was going to found an internet company in China.

It wasn't going smoothly. Ma's first two ventures were failures. But four years later, he managed to convince seventeen of his friends to invest in his vision for an online marketplace. That's how "Alibaba" was born. This site allows sellers to post their products online, and customers can buy them directly. Soon, the service started to attract members from all over the world. By 1999, the company had earned $25 million. Ma maintained a sense of fun and friendship in Alibaba. There are very few employers who would, like him, give each employee a can of Silly String to celebrate a success or encourage the employees to keep their energy up by doing handstands. In 2005, Yahoo invested $1 billion in Alibaba in exchange for a 40% stake in the company. Ma left his post as CEO in 2013, staying on as executive chairman. The company's $150 billion IPO was the largest offering for a company in the history of the New York Stock Exchange. And Ma became the wealthiest man in China, with an estimated worth of $25 billion.

Despite this, Ma maintains modest hobbies, such as reading and writing kung fu fiction, practicing Thai Chi, meditating, and playing poker. He keeps his family life out of the spotlights and encourages his employees to use their wealth to help others, be kind, and live happily.

KFC – Success Story

Do you like chicken dishes from KFC? Have you ever wondered who the old guy on their logo is? It's Colonel Harland Sanders, the founder of Kentucky Fried Chicken. If you are often rejected and feel disappointed, read his story. This extraordinary man was born in 1890 in Henryville, Indiana. When he was six years old, his father passed away, leaving him to care for siblings. In seventh grade, he dropped out of school and left home to work on a farm. At the age of sixteen, he faked his age to enlist in the US army. Because of that lie, he was soon discharged and started working as a labourer on the railway. In that time, he studied law. But, he got fired because of fighting with a colleague. Also because of another fight, he ruined his legal career. The next job, selling life insurance, also failed, because of insubordination.

He founded a ferry boat company and wanted to sell it to create a lamp manufacturer, but do someone already had invented a better version of his lamp. His next venture was buying a motel, which burned to the ground in a fire. Sanders didn't give up, so he rebuilt a new one. Then it came to The World War II, and he had to close it down. After the war, he tried to franchise his restaurant and to sell the recipe but was rejected an incredible 1009 times. Even that didn't discourage him, and he finally succeeded. His "Kentucky Fried Chicken" became a hit fast food chain and expanded internationally. Sanders sold the company for $2 million ($15.3 million today).

Do you still feel that you have tried everything and there is no hope, after reading this?

Part 3. Start your journey to a happy you

Happiness is the Key

Many factors influence one's productivity and a level of enthusiasm. Intuitively, from experience, we know there is some relation between happiness and motivation. When we feel satisfied, we are more likely to be productive. Is that really so?

There is enough evidence to say for sure that happy people are motivated. Happiness positively impacts productivity, many studies have shown. In one of the researches on this topic, it turned out that people who have had some lousy life event in the previous two years had a lower performance by about 10%.

People who found balance and inner peace are enthusiastic. Positive thinking provides us with internal force, and positive expectations make us willing to put an effort in work.

Not only that happiness has a high impact on one's performance, but it also radiates others, and have a significant effect on overall satisfaction at a workplace. Achieving personal happiness improves our relations and all aspects of our lives, not only productivity. That's just one of many reasons to begin your journey to happiness.

All of the said could implicate that only happy people can be productive and good workers. But it's not the whole true. Sad or depressed people can also do their job correctly, but we focus on the level of motivation and enthusiasm here. Motivation and productivity, it turned out, don't depend as much on happiness as they do on positive thinking. A positive approach to life will keep you persistent even when things don't go as you expected. The anticipation of success increases your chances to bring it to the reality.

Take Baby Steps

Many of us know we could improve. We have wishes and dreams, we read about self-development; many of us take some curses, listen to podcasts; we set our goals and write down lists of decisions. We make a decision to start tomorrow, but that tomorrow never comes. Or we keep our promise, and this time stick to the new schedule - for a day, two, a week, but then abandoned a new routine. Why? Because it's overwhelming. It's unnatural. It's too radical.

Self-improvement is so often misunderstood. That doesn't happen overnight, like a switch of a light. It's a journey. A lifetime journey.

We are convinced that there are many quick yet efficient solutions which bring amazing results in just a short time. You want to become fit? There are many diets and workout plans which will do the magic for you, in two weeks, a month, as soon as you want.

If you want to become healthy, there are many pills and plans for your diet, your life routine, and your job is just to apply everything. You want to become happier? Nice, from tomorrow you should behave entirely different and live as you woke up in other's skin. Possible? Hardly. That's why the New Year's resolutions usually fail. Quick solutions are unnatural. That's not how things work.

Drastic overnight changes bring us nothing but more stress to our already stressful lives. What many people overlook searching for quick fixes is that reaching mindfulness and happiness is a journey, not a final destination. Change is a process.
Trying to achieve all and everything at once leads only to burnout and giving up.

But how can you change then? Step by step. Taking small and easily actionable steps will lead you to the best version of yourself and the life you want. Tiny baby steps are not stressful and don't demand you to turn your life upside down. If you take these gentle steps on a regular basis, you are on the right way to succeed. Taking tiny steps each day toward your goal will bring you there, on the opposite of trying to apply everything at once and give up, exhausted.

Your new way of living is nothing but your new habits, little changes, sticking to the new routine, making different choices and decisions. All of that makes a life. All of that happens every day. And you have numerous opportunities to do that the way you want.

What else should you keep on the mind while taking baby steps toward your dreams? Be gentle with yourself. If some step you tend to take makes you feel anxious, consider changing it for a smaller one. You don't need stress, that's the point of making baby steps.

Make it a habit. It's easier if you don't have to think about what you should do the next, or when to do that, and so on. A habit makes you smoothly flow toward your goal, without even thinking about it.

Be consistent. Maybe you have decided to work out fifteen minutes every morning, or reading two pages of a book. Whatever it is, don't skip it any single day. That's how you will progress. Pick just one small thing to change at a time. Don't try to handle many little changes at the same time - that is not taking baby steps. Focus on just one small change until you make it a habit. Then you are ready to go further.

Begin small. We mean very small. If even thinking about going to the gym makes you feel exhausted, start with a walk. Begin with only five minute walk, or even walking through the home.

If you want to improve your health, start with tiny changes, like a small portion of vegetable - a few slices of cucumber is a great start.

You've got it. Take gentle, small steps toward your goals and the change will become obvious.

Start Planning and Get Organized

Productivity depends on efficiency. How efficient you are, depends on how much you can do in a certain amount of time. Time is our precious yet limited resource. That's why we should know how to use it wisely. Time management is an essential skill for achieving success. It involves planning, organizing and prioritizing. There are some simple steps and tips that will help you to plan and organize your time and activities.

1. Make Your To-Do List

Writing down your tasks for each day is a must for productivity. And there are very few things feel better than checking tasks done.

2. Rank Your Tasks.

Not all of the tasks are of the same importance. To prioritize them means to decide which of them are the most important, which are urgent and which can wait. Then do the most important and critical first, then go for the others.

3. Make Schedules and Timetables

That will help you to organize time in a day and to see clearly on what you spend it, is it smart usage or wasting. Sticking to the schedule makes you more productive, avoid procrastination and time wasting.

4. Plan Your Schedule According to Your Energy

Some of us are most productive in the morning, while others are night birds. You know when in a day you are most energized, so try to organize your schedule around your inner clock.

5. Set Realistic Deadlines

If you don't have a limited time to finish a task, you are more likely to procrastinate, and it is more wish than a goal. Your deadlines must be realistic. Otherwise, you won't succeed in respecting them.

6. Take Regular Breaks

Don't even try to make a schedule without pauses counted. It's impossible to keep up with, and if you try, you'll experience all the harmful consequences of burnout.

7. Remove Distractions

Predict what could distract you in finishing work, and try to avoid it. Turn off notifications, social networks, human distractors, stuff around you which take your attention, and adhere to work.

8. Divide Big Tasks into Smaller Ones

A task from your list which seems overwhelming can be chopped to small chunks. Check off every small part as a particular task from your detailed list and enjoy the confidence you find.

9. Use Checklists for Repetitive Tasks

If you are tired or distracted, there are chances to overview something. So follow a checklist for repetitive tasks.

10. Organize Your Space

Cluttered space distracts attention from work. Clean and organize your environment and your virtual space, too. You'll feel light and focused.

11. Prepare for Each Day

If you prepare for the next day, tomorrow you will be thankful for saved energy and effort.

12. Start the Day with Valuable You-Time

Set a morning routine, which makes you feel energized and positively set for the day.

Part 4. Frist Thing's First
Set Your Goals

It's nice to have wishes and daydream about the life you want. It can also help you to bring these dreams to the reality. But it' not even close to enough. Without a plan, effort, and purposeful action, any dream will stay what it is - only a wish. If you want your dream to come true, you need to change it to a goal. What is the difference? Opposite a wish, a goal involves an actionable plan to achieve it. Goal setting is a skill of making an action plan to motivate and guide a person toward a goal. It's a process which encourages you to think about your wanted future and motivate yourself to turn that ideal to the reality.

So, what your ideal future looks like? What do you need to achieve to live such a life? Think about things you want to accomplish to become the best version of yourself. Maybe you want to earn a certain amount of money, to succeed in a career, get a degree, improve your health, find the life partner, travel the world... Everyone has different dreams; you know what are yours. Now, let's change them to goals. What do you need to do to get there? Maybe you need to lose weight, to pass seventeen exams or change your job. Start making a plan. What steps do you need to take to accomplish that huge goal? Break it into smaller parts. For example, if you want to lose 20 pounds, it's a big goal. And it's ok for a long-term goal. But you can divide it into ten smaller goals - to lose 2 pounds. And when you achieve a little goal, then the other, and the next one, you'll feel satisfied and confident. And you'll be able to measure your progress. So, it's important to set both kinds, long-term and short-term goals. The long-term are bigger goals, for which you need more time to achieve. They can be divided into smaller, short-term goals, which will guide you toward the success, motivate you, and show you if you are on the right path.

What does it mean for your daily routine? What do you need to do on a regular basis to achieve your goal? Maybe you need to go running every day if your goal is to run a marathon. And how will you include those activities in your everyday life? That's called a plan. It's wise to predict how much time you will need to succeed and set timeliness according to this factor. Also, to anticipate distractors and obstacles that may occur, and think about possible solutions.

Write down your goal. That simple gesture drastically increases chances to make them happen. Your goals need to be right-sized. That means big enough that it is a challenge and it achieving it is a success for you but still small enough to not make you anxious or overwhelmed.

The goal setting theory says that a goal should be SMART. S is for specific, M for measurable, A for achievable, R for realistic, and T for timely. That's something to keep on mind when planning yours. Specific goals are more precise than general. "I want to lose 20 pounds" is more specific than just "I want to lose weight." That's much easier to imagine, to measure, and to succeed in. Measuring your progress is important. How will you know if you're doing it right and are you getting any closer to your destination? Subjective feeling is unrealistic and often not enough. Of course, your goal needs to be achievable. If you pick something out of your reach, you won't stay motivated for a long. If it's something unachievable, it just isn't a goal, and there's no point in burning out striving for it. That also means you must be realistic when setting goals if you really want to bring your dreams to the reality. And, finally, a goal must have limited time. A deadline or time frame will make you focused in your actions.

We already talked about the importance of setting long-term and short-term goals. The first ones are bigger, complex, and take more time to achieve. The other ones are their components, turned in particular small goals. If we talk about motivation, there's one more thing with these kinds of a goal. From time to time, if you are attached to your big goal, it may cause you to feel overwhelmed, even without real action. The trick is to change the perspective then and to shift your focus. Instead of looking far away, and thinking about your significant achievement and bright future, if you feel pressure, focus on your short-term goals. That will reduce stress and awake motivation while keeping you productive and on the right path toward your goal.

Be realistic. While setting your goals and planning actions, being realistic is very helpful. That means you will choose a realistic goal, which is possible to accomplish. We don't say you should shrink your dreams. Dream big; there's nothing wrong in that, but the goals have to be set in reality. Then, a reasonable time limit will make you put effort and give your best. Also, it keeps it realistic. You need both feet on the ground when thinking about yourself and your possibilities. Do you have all the skills and knowledge necessary for achieving the goal? Maybe you should improve some of that? Sincerely look at your strong sides, but at your weaknesses, too. Be honest with yourself. Only that way, you'll have a real picture. That will save you a lot of energy and time, and help you to avoid unnecessary disappointment.

Make a To-Do List

If you often happen to forget to do something or have a feeling you are unorganized, you probably are. Also, if you happen to miss the deadlines, or people need to remind you of things, you probably don't make to-do lists or don't use it the right way. A to-do list is a list of all the tasks you need to carry out, written in one place. Your list should be prioritized, which means that tasks are listed by importance - from most important and urgent, to the least.

Having such a list makes you sure you won't miss any task, helps you stay focused and organized. It improves your motivation and increases productivity. This way, you won't find yourself wasting the whole day doing laundry while your presentation for tomorrow is not ready. How can you make a proper to-do list for the best results?

1.   Choose a medium and write down your tasks

Write all the tasks waiting for you. Writing by hand is the best for remembering, but if you're not familiar with a pen anymore, it's ok to use some of many applications for making to-do lists.

2.   Having a few lists is ok

You don't have to clog your list with all the wishes, New Year resolutions, daily tasks, mixed with those waiting for ten years. Having a few separated lists is ok- a master list with all the wishes and long-term goals, a weekly list of tasks, and a daily - with only the duties you are going to finish that day.

3. Keep it short and straightforward

Limit the number of items on the list to ideally six, anyway not more than ten. Miles long lists make you feel tired just of looking at them.

4. Prioritize

If all the tasks on the list have the same importance, that's a recipe for disaster. That's the same as if you say none of them matters. So, make priorities - from the most important at the top, to less significant.

5. Simple tasks are ok, but be careful

Checking off from your list simple everyday tasks as taking a shower or washing dishes will make you feel super-productive. Just be careful not to clutter your list with unnecessary items and to set priorities correctly.

6. Break it down

A colossal task makes you afraid even to start. So break it down into smaller bites you would be able to check done one by one.

7. Be specific

Each task needs to be specific, physical action, which can be finished in one sitting, and requires you to do it.

8. Time it

When you set a specific time for each task, you turn your list into a schedule. There is a time for each activity, and when it's over, it's over, and the work should be done.

9. Set it visible

Put your list in a visible place, like a refrigerator, a wall, or somewhere it will be on your sight to remain you.

10. Remain with the old

The list of all the tasks you managed to finish and check done will make you confident and remain you how super-productive you are.

11. Start fresh

New day - a new list. Make a fresh list for each day.

12. Be flexible, don't stress, and relax

Don't stress yourself about checking off items from the list. It's no point in living in the list and calendar. It's here only to serve you and help you be as productive as you possibly can. Leave some spare space in your schedule for rest and joy, and put on your list some "tasks" which are wishes in fact and make you happy.

Before making your to-do list, wait for a moment; ask yourself the important questions - what do you need to get a task done; how much time do you need, what logistics do you need? Maybe you need someone's help, perhaps to delegate others for some tasks. Do you have all the tools required and supplies? Enough space? Prepare in advance so you won't waste the time of really doing work. How much time would it take you to finish the task? Be realistic, count all the possible circumstances, include regular pauses. When you have all these factors on your mind, you have more realistic expectations of yourself and won't have to struggle with overviewed obstacles. Set small milestones and achieve them.

As you successfully go down the list, your productivity will automatically improve. Every checked task gives you confidence, no matter how little it is. If you have divided your responsibility for small milestones, every achieved milestone makes you closer to the finished work. Every small success counts and assures you that you are on the right way, you are skilled enough, you do it right. Many people think that motivation comes before productivity. The truth is that seeing yourself being productive is incredibly motivating. It affects each other, and you can be sure both, your motivation and productivity will increase as you go through your daily to-do list.

Because we are emotional beings, don't forget to reward yourself for being productive, and to celebrate every victory, no matter how small the improvement is. Small incentives and rewards will make you always have something to looking forward to, even if it's just a cup of a favorite coffee during a pause, or spa weekend after the long work week. Be proud of yourself and your improvement, celebrate your success and remind yourself how much you deserve it.

Part 5. Hacks for Staying Happy, Motivated, and Productive

When you feel you are losing your courage and motivation and your work/productivity starts to suffer then you need to take action.

1.   Procrastination is not your friend

If you say enough times: "I finished the work. I finished the work", would it really finish by itself? The same thing is with procrastinating. If you wait for long enough, would your task finish by itself? Of course not. So, you have to wade into the work. If you are waiting to feel motivated, you could sit still for good. It will hardly ever show up if you don't take some action. As more time goes by, you are further from it, because procrastination keeps it away. We already wrote about procrastination. Now it's your turn to kick it and become proactive and efficient. So, bite the bullet! At the beginning of the workday, do the hardest, most unpleasant task waiting for you. Don't put it on hold, do that chore right now. Wash the dishes - now, not later. Do the laundry. Do those evil squads and jumping jacks. Work out for 15 minutes - start now. Pick up the phone and make the call you are avoiding for so long. Being productive starts now. Everything we already talked about, including to-do lists and goal setting will help you to stop procrastinating and make the best usage of your time.

2.   Lazy body, lazy mind – stay active

The best way to awake your lethargic spirit is to jump out of bed and work out. Run around the house or do some push-ups.

You'll feel the energy flow, and you'll awaken and be motivated in a moment. Also, it's the best way to take maximum from your pauses. Use a breather from work to do planks, or stretching, and you'll find out it's the best way to use the break smartly. Accomplishing a daily work-out routine is an excellent way to keep your energy high. You'll experience many benefits of that - health improvement, great figure, high energy, motivation, and productivity. So, put your running sneakers on!

3. Deal with and remove all negative factors from your personal and professional environment

Remove all negative factors from your personal and professional environment. Well, it's not always possible to obliterate them, we know. If you have a colleague you don't go well with, or you have to do a job you don't love for a living, you can't altogether avoid that. Maybe you are not satisfied with some of your life circumstances. You are working hard to change the situation, but you should find a way to be happy and productive in the meantime, too, until the change happens. If you can't change something you don't like in your reality at this point, there's always something completely under your control - that's your point of view and your focus. You can choose your thoughts and feelings, and you are the one who decide how your life looks like. When it's about factors you can control, try to remove from your environment everything that keeps you from being motivated, cheerful and energized. Avoid hanging with people who make you feel drained. Remove all the clutter from your space. Change bad habits, which are harmful to your body, mind or spirit. Free up the space for new good things - make some free time for things you want to do, some space in your schedule for people who inspire you, room in your house for activities. Think about all kind of things that affect your enthusiasm and efficiency negatively and then don't hesitate to remove them without guilt.

4.   Yes, it is important to read and get new ideas

We could talk for ages about the incredible effects of reading. You can't expect from your mind to perfectly perform if you feed it with worthless garbage. As every system in nature or technique, our brain needs quality input. It's essential what with you are feeding it. Reading will improve your imagination and creativity. If you choose the right books to read, you can gain knowledge and get inspiration. Books also can motivate and encourage you; spending time reading is also energizing like meditation. You need new ideas, new points of view, new concepts and fresh thoughts for your mind if you want to keep it awake and active. So, make yourself a cup of coffee or tea, open a book, and enjoy.

5.   Make time for the all-important "me time"

It's not selfish. It's necessary. If you continuously spend energy but don't recharge, burnout is close. And if that happens, you will need much more time to recover and get back on the track, than if you spent some time on your wellbeing. So, reserve some time only for yourself. It's crucial to be alone sometimes, to get rest and enough sleep, enjoy the activities you love, and be kind to yourself. Reward yourself not only for achievements but for the effort you made. Use your "me-time" wisely, not pushing yourself with just another kind of to-do list. Slow down, pick only one or two activities which energize you and enjoy. Being alone is sometimes the best possible choice.

6. Eat healthy.

While you work on your motivation and productivity, focusing on your mind, it's important not to forget the body, too. Because we are all of that in one - mind, body, and spirit. You can't be completely satisfied if any of that is not in good condition. Just like our mind, the body needs quality input to give us back in health and abilities. If you didn't pay attention to what you are taking in, now it's time to begin. You should hydrate enough, drinking at least two litres of water. When it's about food, your body needs balanced meals, with enough fresh fruits and vegetables. It's important to include enough proteins and carbohydrates. Five meals, with no skipping, will make your metabolism fast enough to keep balance in your body. If you are overweight or have some eating issue, it's important to talk to a nutritionist, and find a special diet to solve it. The right food is for our body the same as fuel for the engine. So, don't underestimate this significant factor of well-being.

Conclusion

Now, if you have read carefully and applied all of the advice from the book, nothing can stop you. You know how to awake and maintain motivation, what to do when enthusiasm fades away, and how to make yourself get off your butt and achieve your goals. You are a pro at setting goals and making to-do lists. If you apply our hacks and tricks for achieving happiness, you are on the right way to become the best version of yourself and live your dream life. When you live your life to the fullest and enjoy every single day, the productivity follows; your life is meaningful, and you have a sense of purpose.

So, what now? Now you are ready. Develop your new routine, think about habits you want to maintain and which will lead you, step by step, to your goal. Think about your goals, make a clear vision of what you wish to, and exact plan of gentle steps you are going to take. There's no need to rush. Start small and slow, but stick to your decision to succeed. That way, this is going to be an incredible journey.

www.ingramcontent.com/pod-product-compliance
Lightning Source LLC
Chambersburg PA
CBHW070958240526
45469CB00016B/1618